GOD AND ME

Preschool TeamKID Activity Book

Written by

KATRI WHITLOCK   RICHARD SHAHAN   AMY MORROW

Illustrated by

SUSAN HARRISON

Convention Press
Nashville, Tennessee

© Copyright 1995 • Convention Press

All rights reserved
Nashville, Tennessee
5200-95
ISBN: 0-8054-9544-4

DEWEY: 268.432
SUBHD: DISCIPLESHIP TRAINING—PRESCHOOLERS
Printed in the United States of America

Children/Preschool Section
Youth/Children/Preschool Department
Discipleship and Family Development Division
The Sunday School Board of the Southern Baptist Convention
127 Ninth Avenue, North
Nashville, Tennessee 37234
Melanie Allbritten Williams, Editor
Paula Savage, Art Director
Synnove Inman, Graphic Designer

Scripture quotations marked (NIV) are from the Holy Bible, *New International Version*.
Copyright © 1973, 1978, 1984 by International Bible Society. Used by permission.

Scripture quotations marked (GNB) are from Today's English Version.
Copyright © American Bible Society 1966, 1971, 1976 1992.
Used by permission.

Contents

A Welcome Word to Parents

We are happy your child is a part of our Preschool TeamKID club. We want to work with you in promoting the spiritual development of your child. Our prayer is that the materials and suggested activities in Preschool TeamKID will nurture your child's spiritual and moral development.

The activity pages your child will bring home are designed to support what he or she has learned during the meeting. There may not have been enough time for your child to have participated in all the suggested activities. We hope you will work with your child on the activities he or she has not already experienced. You can also extend your child's learning by talking about the Bible verses he or she heard during the meeting, which are listed on the activity sheet.

Please encourage your child to talk about what he or she learned during the meeting. Let the time you spend with your child on these activities be a time in which you learn together.

The World God Made

Provide pictures of flowers cut from seed catalogs.
Guide preschoolers to glue the pictures in the meadow below.
Set out crayons or water-based markers and encourage
the preschoolers to draw more things God made.

7

God Made It Mini Mural

PROVIDE

strips of 12-by-24-inch art paper (one per child), crayons or water-based markers

WHAT TO DO

Say, "The Bible says that 'God... made the world and everything in it.'" Ask the preschoolers to tell you some things God made. Guide them to draw on their mini murals different things God made.

Play Dough Surprise

PROVIDE

play dough, resealable bags

WHAT TO DO

Make individual balls for the preschoolers and poke a hole in each ball with your little finger. Put two drops of food coloring in each hole and pinch the hole together. Place each ball in a resealable bag. Talk about the surprises God gives us to enjoy, like a seed growing and becoming a flower. Tell the preschoolers to leave their play dough in the bags and slowly knead it. Soon they will be surprised that their play dough changes colors! Encourage them to take the play dough out and make their own creations.

Nature Painting

PROVIDE

nature items such as: a stick, a flower, a pine cone; two colors of tempera paint in shallow pans; sheets of newsprint or large construction paper; painting smocks

WHAT TO DO

Guide the preschoolers to paint or print designs with various nature items. Remind them of the beautiful things God made.

Cooked Play Dough

1 cup flour
1 cup water
2 tsp cream of tartar
food coloring (optional)
½ cup salt
1 Tbs cooking oil

Mix all dry ingredients. Add cooking oil, water, and food coloring. Cook in an electric skillet on low heat, stirring constantly until mixture thickens and becomes one large ball. This should take no more than 3 minutes. Empty onto waxed paper and knead until smooth. Store in a plastic bowl with a lid or a resealable bag.

Parents!

Your child may have participated in any one of these activities during this meeting. You can extend your child's learning by working with him or her on these activities at home. You can also talk about the Bible verses which your child heard during the meeting: "God...made the world and everything in it." Acts 17:24 (GNB); "God saw all that he had made, and it was very good." Genesis 1:31 (NIV); "He has made everything beautiful." Ecclesiastes 3:11 (NIV).

Day In, Day Out

Set out crayons or water-based markers. Guide the preschoolers to circle
all the pictures of activities done at night. Say the Bible verse "God called
light 'day,' and the darkness he called 'night.'" (Genesis 1:5)

9

Nighttime Quilt

PROVIDE

fabric squares (approx. 2 by 2 inches) in various colors and designs, glue, construction paper, a quilt or picture of a quilt

WHAT TO DO

Show the preschoolers the quilt or picture of a quilt. Explain to them that quilts keep people warm at night. Guide them to notice the different patterns and designs. Allow them to create their own quilts from materials you have provided.

Pillow Talk

PROVIDE

a pillowcase with the following items inside: toothbrush, small stuffed animal, tube of toothpaste, spoon, fork, candle, bath cloth, fresh bar of soap

WHAT TO DO

Use the pillowcase for a "feely" bag. Tell the preschoolers the bag contains different things that may be used at night. Explain to them that they can put one hand in the bag and try to guess what one of the objects is without looking. When a preschooler correctly guesses the item, show the object and discuss its nighttime use.

Parents!

Your child may have participated in any one of these activities during this meeting. You can extend your child's learning by working with him or her on these activities at home. You can also talk about the Bible verses which your child heard during the meeting: "God called light 'day,' and the darkness he called 'night.'" Genesis 1:5 (NIV); "God saw all that he had made, and it was very good." Genesis 1:31 (NIV); "He has made everything beautiful." Ecclesiastes 3:11 (NIV).

Night Clouds

PROVIDE

white chalk, black paper, a cup of water, a brush approximately ½ to 1 inch wide

WHAT TO DO

Tell the preschoolers to brush water across the entire surface of a sheet of black construction paper. While the paper is still wet, the preschoolers may draw clouds with white chalk. Talk about how God made different kinds of clouds—some are light and airy, some are dark and heavy and bring lots of rain. Include in your conversation the Bible verses for this meeting.

UNIT TWO
MEETING ONE

What's Out of Place?

Provide pencils and water-based markers or crayons. Guide the boys and girls to look carefully at the picture. Ask them to identify any animals that do not belong under the sea by circling them with a pencil. After they have located all five, guide them to mark the various creatures that ARE part of the ocean with a marker or crayon. Talk about all of the different kinds of animals that live in the ocean and the fact that God made each one different.

19

Looking Through a Porthole

PROVIDE

heavy-duty paper plate, water-based markers or crayons, sand, shells (or construction paper to tear into shell shapes), green chenille craft stems, gel glue, paintbrush for gluing, blue plastic wrap, clear tape

WHAT TO DO

Tell the boys and girls to pretend they are in a submarine under water, looking out of the portholes (or windows). Explain that they are going to make a picture of what they are "seeing." Guide them to draw 2 or 3 animals they "see" on the paper plate (their porthole). Guide them to use a paintbrush to spread glue across the bottom of the plate. Direct them to sprinkle sand on the glue and add shells or tear shell shapes out of construction paper and glue them on the sand. They can make seaweed with 2- to 3-inch pieces of green craft stems. Help a child to lay a piece of blue plastic wrap flat on the table. Then turn the plate facedown in the middle of the plastic wrap and bring the edges over the back of the plate and tape them in place with transparent tape.

Going Fishing

PROVIDE

sponges cut in fish and sea animal shapes, dishpan, fish net or kitchen strainer, blue construction paper, tempera paint (2 or 3 light colors), painting smocks, pie pans, paper towels (for each color of paint)

WHAT TO DO

Place sponge shapes in a dishpan of water. Allow children to "scoop" out a fish with the net then wring the water from the sponge completely. Place a paper towel in the bottom of a pie pan. Pour a little paint on the towel, creating a "stamp pad" for them to press their sponges on. Guide the children to make a picture using their shapes (washing them out between colors or trading shapes with their friends.)

Crayon Resist Ocean Scene

PROVIDE

12-by-18-inch white art paper cut in half lengthwise, crayons, 2-inch sponge brush, blue tempera paint (very thin color, more water that normal)

WHAT TO DO

Guide preschoolers to draw an underwater scene with the crayons. Show them how to draw with heavy lines. Suggest that they add various animals, fish, plants, shells, and so forth. When they complete their drawings, they can take turns using the sponge brush to paint the blue wash lightly over the entire paper. The crayon will resist the paint and shine through.

Parents!

Your child has participated in some of these activities during this meeting. You can extend your child's learning by working with him or her on these activities at home. You can also talk about the Bible verses which your child heard during the meeting: "God created the great creatures of the sea." Genesis 1:21 (NIV); "Give thanks to the Lord, for He is good." Psalm 107:1 (NIV); "I will sing to the Lord." Exodus 15:1 (NIV).

Complete the Picture

Provide pencils and water-based markers or crayons. Guide the boys and girls to complete the picture on the right side of the paper. The picture on the left side gives them a suggestion of how to complete the bird, butterfly, and bee. After completing their drawings, they may choose to add additional items around them (clouds, flowers, trees, and so forth).

21

Birds in Flight

PROVIDE

large drawing paper (12-by-18-inch), crayons, water colors, painting smocks, cardboard or poster board

The Many Colors of Birds

PROVIDE

drawing paper, colored chalk, cotton balls, cardboard stencils, masking tape, pump hair spray

WHAT TO DO

Use the leftover part of the cardboard from "Birds in Flight" as a stencil (have one for each child). Guide the preschoolers to tape the stencil on a piece of drawing paper. (Tape the paper to the table.) Explain to the boys and girls how to rub a cotton ball against the side of a piece of chalk and then on the paper inside the stencil to form the bird's wings. When they have finished, remove the stencil and help the child spray the picture with hair spray. (Placing the paper in the bottom of a box will help to contain the spray.)

WHAT TO DO

Before the meeting use the bird shape from around this activity to cut out a pattern for each child from cardboard. Tell the children to imagine they are in the sky, flying with the birds. They are going to make a picture of what they see. Help them to place their bird pattern on the paper and trace around it with a crayon. Repeat this process 3 to 5 times, using a different colored crayon each time (it is all right if the wings overlap). After tracing around the pattern, guide them to paint their birds, matching the color of crayon and paint. Colors will blend where the wings overlap. As they paint, tell them about birds and how some fly in groups called flocks.

Butterfly Place Mat

PROVIDE

butterfly frames (enlarge the pattern below and cut it out of black construction paper; you may want to do 2 to 3 in different sizes for each child), blunt-nosed scissors, clear self-adhesive plastic (two 9-by-18-inch pieces per child), hole punch, construction paper pieces

WHAT TO DO

Talk about the variety of colors and markings on butterflies. Explain how God uses those colors to help butterflies hide from other animals that would hurt them. Guide each child to make some confetti by punching holes in the construction paper. Help each child lay one piece of the clear self-adhesive plastic flat on the table in front of her, sticky side up. She can place her butterfly frames wherever she chooses (even if the wings overlap). Instruct her to sprinkle confetti on the wing sections of the butterflies. Help her seal the place mat by putting on the second piece of self-adhesive plastic. Edges can be trimmed if not aligned exactly.

Parents!

Your child may have participated in some of these activities during this meeting. You can extend your child's learning by working with him or her on these activities at home. You can also talk about the Bible verses which your child heard during the meeting: "God created...all kinds of birds." Genesis 1:21 (NIV); "Give thanks to the Lord, for He is good." Psalm 107:1 (NIV); "I will sing to the Lord." Exodus 15:1 (NIV).

What Do These Animals Provide for Us?

Provide pencils, water-based markers, and crayons.
Guide the boys and girls to draw a line from the animal to what it
provides for people to use. When they finish, they may
choose to draw additional animals. Talk about how God provides
for us through the various animals He created.

25

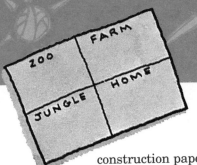

What Kind of Animal Is It?

PROVIDE

construction paper, crayons or water-based markers, scissors, magazine pages with animal pictures, envelopes

WHAT TO DO

Before the meeting divide each sheet of paper into four sections with a marker and write these words, one per section: *zoo, farm, jungle, home.* Tell the preschoolers they are going to make a game they can share with others at home. Give each child a sheet of the paper you have prepared and tell her to illustrate a cage (for *zoo*); a barn (for *farm*); trees (for *jungle*); a house (for *home*). Lay out the magazine pages you brought and tell the preschoolers to select 2 to 3 animals for each category. Direct them to cut around each animal's picture. Talk with them about where the animals may live, making sure they understand the animals can probably live in several different places. When they are finished, guide them to play the game. They can keep their pictures in the envelope to take home with them.

Animal Construction

WHAT TO DO

Guide preschoolers to create an animal from straw pieces and masking tape. Help them cut the straws into various lengths as needed. They can use small balls of play dough to anchor the "animal" to the table. They may choose to make an animal you have talked about, or they may want to create some new, "never-before-seen" animals. They can take their creations home on the cardboard squares.

PROVIDE

drinking straws (straight and bendable), scissors, masking tape, small balls of play dough, cardboard squares

Animal Tracks

PROVIDE

heavy-duty paper plate for each child, play dough, pencils, toothpicks, a variety of animal pictures

WHAT TO DO

Talk about the many different kinds of feet animals have. They are different in size, shape, and appearance. Guide the preschoolers to cover the paper plates with a thin layer of play dough. Then let them practice making "tracks" across their plates. Generate discussion and actions by suggesting, "What would a rabbit's (or an elephant's, dog's, chicken's, etc.) tracks look like?" To make tracks, boys and girls may choose to use the eraser of a pencil, toothpicks, or their fingers. They can "flatten" the tracks and start over as many times as they desire.

Parents!

Your child has participated in some of these activities during this meeting. You can extend your child's learning by working with him or her on these activities at home. You can also talk about the Bible verses which your child heard during the meeting: "So He took some soil from the ground and formed all the animals and all the birds. Then he brought them to [Adam] to see what he would name them; and that is how they all got their names." Genesis 2:19-20 (GNB); "Give thanks to the Lord, for He is good." Psalm 107:1 (NIV); "I will sing to the Lord." Exodus 15:1 (NIV).

Where Is My Home?

Provide blunt-nosed scissors and glue. Guide boys and girls to cut apart the animals at the bottom of the page. They can match the animal to its home by gluing it to the appropriate picture. Talk about how we can take care of the places the animals call home.

Animal Bodies

PROVIDE

construction paper, cardboard, crayons or water-based markers, scissors, clothespins, animal shape cut-outs (use the shapes around the instructions on this page)

WHAT TO DO

Before the meeting enlarge the animal shapes on this page to approximately six or seven inches across. Cut two of each out of cardboard. Most five-year-olds will be able to trace around the outside of the shape; three-year-olds can trace around the inside of the shape (the "left-overs" after you cut out the shape). Allow each child to trace and cut out all three of the animal shapes, or if they choose, they can draw the body of an animal without using the shapes. Guide them to color them, adding eyes, mouths, and other features. Boys and girls can make their animals stand up by attaching clothespins upside down at the appropriate locations. Talk about the different sounds each animal makes.

A Rainbow Book of Animals

PROVIDE

construction paper (cut in half, 3–4 pieces per child), hole punch, yarn, blunt-nosed scissors, gel glue, magazine pictures of animals

WHAT TO DO

Guide the preschoolers to stack their construction paper halves on top of each other and punch two holes on the left side. Help them tie a piece of yarn through the holes, creating a booklet. Next, direct the preschoolers to look through the magazine pictures you have brought and locate animals they would like to include in their booklets. They can cut around the animal and glue it to the appropriate page (perhaps matching the color of the animals to the pages). They may wish to decorate their booklets or color around their pictures.

God Made a Rainbow

PROVIDE

drawing paper, water-based markers or crayons (red, orange, yellow, green, blue, purple), construction paper pieces (in the same colors), gel glue

WHAT TO DO

Guide preschoolers to draw a rainbow, making one arc across the page with each marker or crayon. Tell the boys and girls to tear the construction paper into little pieces, making a little pile of each color in front of them. Help them run a bead of glue between the arcs, one at a time, and to fill that space with the same color of construction paper pieces (for instance, red should fill the space between the red and orange arcs and so on). Discuss the significance of the rainbow; it can remind us today that God will always take care of us.

Parents!

Your child has participated in some of these activities during this meeting.

You can extend your child's learning by working with him or her on these activities at home. You can also talk about the Bible verses which your child heard during the meeting: "Noah did everything just as God commanded him." Genesis 6:22 (NIV); "Give thanks to the Lord, for He is good." Psalm 107:1 (NIV); "I will sing to the Lord." Exodus 15:1 (NIV).

I Am Special

Provide crayons, water-based markers, and pencils. Talk about
the special bodies God gave us. Point out characteristics that make us
unique. Ask preschoolers to draw pictures of themselves.

"You created every part of me." (Psalm 139:13)

Hug Me Doll

PROVIDE

one white sock for each child, water-based markers, yarn, pillow stuffing or material scraps

WHAT TO DO

Place the art materials on a table or floor. Provide each child with a sock and enough stuffing to fill the foot part of the sock. Show the preschoolers how to stuff the sock, then tie a knot using the sock end. Girls may want to tie a bow for a hair ribbon at the toe of the sock. Use markers to add facial features. When dolls are complete, ask preschoolers to give their dolls a big hug!

Me Posters

PROVIDE

poster board, water-based markers, crayons, glue, rickrack, buttons, construction paper, old magazines, scissors, hole punch, yarn

WHAT TO DO

Cut poster board into four equal pieces. Provide one piece for each child. Print *My Me Poster* at the bottom of each piece. Place art materials in the center of the work area. You may want to suggest to the preschoolers to draw a picture of themselves, write their names, cut out their favorite foods or toys from the magazines, and use the rickrack and buttons for borders or making designs). Preschoolers can hang their posters by punching two holes in the top corners and stringing yarn through the holes.

Trace Around Me

PROVIDE

large sheets of art paper, water-based markers, crayons

WHAT TO DO

Cut art paper in strips as long as preschoolers are tall. Place paper and markers on the floor. When preschoolers join you for the activity, ask them to find a partner. They can take turns tracing each other on the paper. Threes may need a coach's help. As you are working, talk about the different characteristics of each child. Suggest that they draw their facial features, hair, clothes, and shoes. They may want to display their drawings.

Measure Me

PROVIDE

Adding machine tape, water-based markers

WHAT TO DO

Ask preschoolers to choose a partner. Each friend will measure the other friend with the adding machine tape. Allow preschoolers to draw pictures of things they enjoy doing or make designs on their strips. Some preschoolers may enjoy finding things that are the same length as their strips.

Parents!

Your child may have participated in any one of these activities during this meeting. You can extend your child's learning by working with him or her on these activities. You can also talk about the Bible verses which your child heard during the meeting: "You created every part of me." Psalm 139:13 (GNB); "He made us, and we belong to him." Psalm 100:3 (GNB); "[Jesus said,] 'I love you.'" John 15:9 (GNB).

UNIT THREE
MEETING THREE

Soft or Hard?

Set out glue, soft items (such as cotton balls, fabric scraps, pieces of ribbon, strips of gauze), and hard items (such as craft sticks, small pebbles, dried beans, acorns, watermelon seeds). Place these materials in the center of the table mixed together. Before preschoolers begin, talk about the words soft and hard. Guide preschoolers to decide if each item is soft or hard and glue it on the correct side of the paper. Talk about how we use our hands to decide if something is soft or hard. Ask preschoolers to describe other ways we use our hands.

  Soft    Hard

35

Sand Paper Art

PROVIDE

sheets of soft- or medium-grade sandpaper, colored chalk, water, pie tins

WHAT TO DO

Fill pie tins with a small amount of water. Before preschoolers begin to draw, ask them to feel the surface of the sandpaper. Talk about how it feels and compare it to the way the chalk feels. Tell preschoolers to dip their chalk into the water before they draw on the sandpaper. Ask, "What's different about sandpaper art?"

Hidden Pictures

PROVIDE

animal stencils and shape stencils (or poster board), crayons, art paper, manila paper

WHAT TO DO

Cut animal outlines and a variety of shapes from poster board or purchase precut stencils. Tape the stencils at various places on a tabletop and cover with a sheet of art paper. Secure the art paper with tape. Remove the wrappers from the crayons. Tell preschoolers to place their paper anywhere on the table and rub firmly with the side of the crayon. Ask them to try to guess what the hidden picture will be.

My Hands Can

PROVIDE

paper sack for each child, recycled art materials (like fabric and paper scraps, sheets of construction paper, yarn, string, tissue paper, wall paper, confetti), art tools (like tape, glue, stapler, hole punch)

WHAT TO DO

Place various art materials in each paper sack and staple it closed. Place art tools on the table. Tell each preschooler to choose a sack and make something from whatever he or she finds in the sack. Encourage preschoolers to be creative. Include in your conversation reminders of ways we use our hands. Draw preschoolers' attention to the way they are using their hands.

Parents!

Your child may have participated in any one of these activities during this meeting. You can extend your child's learning by working with him or her on these activities. You can also talk about the Bible verses which your child heard during the meeting: "Work with you hands." 1 Thessalonians 4:11 (NIV); "He made us, and we belong to him." Psalm 100:3 (GNB); "[Jesus said,] 'I love you.'" John 15:9 (GNB).

My Amazing Ears

Set out crayons. Talk to the preschoolers about how important their ears are. Ask them to name some things they hear all the time. Talk about the difference between loud and soft sounds. Help them through the maze (if needed) and ask them to tell whether each picture shows a loud or soft sound (or both).

37

Ear Phones

PROVIDE
paper cups, hole punch, chenille craft stems, crayons

WHAT TO DO
Give each preschooler two cups. Punch a hole in one side of each cup. (Some preschoolers will be able to do this by themselves.) Attach a craft stem through the holes on either side of the cups. (Two craft stems may be needed.) Preschoolers can place the cups on their ears with the craft stems across the top of their heads, making a set of earphones. Talk with them about how they use their ears.

Listening Tubes

PROVIDE
empty cardboard tubes; water-based markers; paper bag; various nature items such as: rock, shell, feather, pine branch, leaves, acorns

WHAT TO DO
Before the meeting place the nature items in the paper bag. Tell boys and girls they are going to make a listening tube. Invite preschoolers to decorate their tubes with the markers. After decorating, tell preschoolers to place the tubes over one ear and close their eyes. Remove a nature item from the bag and tap it on the table or floor. Ask boys and girls to listen through their tubes and guess the name of the nature item. You may need to give some clues as to where the item is found (and maybe include the color). Discuss the differences in the sounds that the items make.

Musical Instruments

PROVIDE
shoe box lids, rubber bands of various thicknesses, empty coffee cans with lids, paper plates, stapler, dried beans, crayons or water-based markers, hole punch, several colors of paper ribbon

WHAT TO DO
Guide preschoolers to make stringed instruments, drums, or tambourines from the materials listed. To make a stringed instrument: color the inside of a shoe box lid, then wrap five or six rubber bands around it about two inches apart. Plucking the rubber bands makes an interesting sound. To make a drum: decorate plain paper and cover a coffee can with it. To make a tambourine: decorate two paper plates, place beans inside them, and staple them together. For added decoration, punch four holes along the outer edge of the tambourine and thread colored ribbon through them and tie it in a bow. Preschoolers may enjoy moving to the instrumental music and playing their instruments.

Parents!

Your child may have participated in any one of these activities during this meeting. You can extend your child's learning by working with him or her on these activities. You can also talk about the Bible verses which your child heard during the meeting: "The Lord has given us...ears to listen with." Proverbs 20:12 (GNB); "He made us, and we belong to him." Psalm 100:3 (GNB); "[Jesus said,] 'I love you.'" John 15:9 (GNB).

UNIT THREE
MEETING FIVE

Name That Smell

Provide crayons or water-based markers. Talk to preschoolers about things that we smell with our noses. Read the riddle to preschoolers and see if they can guess the picture the riddle is about. Children may want to draw a line from the riddle to the matching picture.

1. I bloom lovely, red, and green,
   But my thorns are really mean!
   Who am I?

2. I am filled with trash and old wood.
   My smell is not too good!
   Who am I?

3. I am black, white, and furry.
   If you see me, better hurry!
   Who am I?

4. Smelling me will bring delight.
   You can eat me for dinner tonight.
   Who am I?

5. Smelling me may not be good.
   Unless it is from the fireplace wood.
   Who am I?

39

Scented Play Dough

PROVIDE

play dough, cookie cutters, scissors, electric skillet

WHAT TO DO

Before the meeting make scented play dough: 1 cup flour; ½ cup salt; 2 teaspoons cream of tartar; 1 tablespoon cooking oil; 1 cup water; 1 teaspoon cloves or cinnamon. Stir constantly over medium heat until play dough forms a ball. Cool and knead. Store in a covered container. Help preschoolers discover the scent of the play dough. Ask questions like: "Do you notice something different about this play dough?" "What color is the play dough?" "What does it smell like?"

Whose Nose?

PROVIDE

paper plates, glue, water-based markers, pictures of noses cut from magazines

WHAT TO DO

Cut lots of noses from magazines before the meeting. These should be both animal and human noses. Place art materials on the table and guide preschoolers to make faces with the paper plates. Preschoolers will enjoy making up silly faces to go with the noses.

Talk about the likenesses and differences in human and animal noses and the ways we each use our noses.

Flower Prints

PROVIDE

fresh leaves and flowers, heavy white paper, hammers, wooden boards, tape

WHAT TO DO

Direct preschoolers to create arrangements of leaves and flowers on their boards. When each is satisfied with his arrangement, help him tape a piece of paper to the board over the flowers. Tell him to hammer all over the paper, crushing the leaves and flowers, then remove the paper and look at the prints left on the paper. *Variation:* Instead of hammering a print, make a rubbing with a peeled crayon or piece of charcoal.

CAUTION

Be sure to ask parents about any allergies to the flowers. Offer another activity if any preschooler has a related allergy.

Parents!

Your child may have participated in any one of these activities during this meeting. You can extend your child's learning by working with him or her on these activities. You can also talk about the Bible verses which your child heard during the meeting: "I praise you because I am...wonderfully made." Psalm 139:14 (NIV); "He made us, and we belong to him." Psalm 100:3 (GNB); "[Jesus said,] 'I love you.'" John 15:9 (GNB).

What Can I Eat?

Provide crayons or water-based markers. Guide preschoolers to identify each picture and decide if it is a picture of something that is safe to put in your mouth. If it is not, tell them to draw an *X* over the picture. If it is not a safe item, talk about why it is not.

41

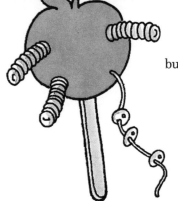

Fruit Stick Puppets

PROVIDE

buttons; craft sticks; hole punch; glue; crayons; a variety of fruit shapes cut from poster board such as: apple, pear, banana; yarn

WHAT TO DO

Cut fruit shapes from poster board before the meeting. Let preschoolers punch holes in each fruit shape where "arms' and "legs" might go. Invite them to decorate their fruit puppets with crayons, buttons, and yarn. To make arms and legs, they can thread four buttons with a 5-inch piece of yarn and string through each hole. Glue a craft stick on the back for a handle to hold the puppet. Talk with preschoolers about the good foods they have to eat, like fruit. They may want to put on a short "play" about good foods to eat.

Toothbrush Painting

PROVIDE

toothbrush for every color of paint; various colors of tempera paint; small, nonbreakable containers for the paint; manila paper

WHAT TO DO

Mix tempera paint and pour into containers. Place toothbrushes in each color of paint. Preschoolers can experiment using the brush in different ways on their paper. Talk about how important is it to brush our teeth and eat good foods to keep our teeth healthy.

I'm Thankful Tree

PROVIDE

large sheet of art paper, masking tape, 8½-by-11-inch manila paper, crayons or markers, glue, scissors

WHAT TO DO

Draw a large tree on the art paper and tape it on the wall. Print at the top of the paper *Our Thankful Tree*. Cut apple shapes from the manila paper, making them as large as you can. Before beginning the activity, talk about things we are thankful for that we can do with our mouths. Include ideas such as: eating, singing, praying, talking, whistling, blowing bubbles, whispering, and shouting. Ask each child to draw something on an apple that he or she is thankful for about mouths. (Threes may want to color the apple.) Glue the apples to the tree.

Blow Painting

PROVIDE

straws, tempera paint, manila paper, plastic spoons

WHAT TO DO

Mix tempera paint to a very very thin consistency. Ask preschoolers to spoon a small amount of several colors of paint on their paper. Demonstrate how to blow through the straw to make the paint move. The colors mix to make a beautiful design. Talk about how God has made our mouths so we can use them in many different ways. Ask preschoolers to think of other ways we can use our mouths.

Parents!

Your child may have participated in any one of these activities during this meeting. You can extend your child's learning by working with him or her on these activities. You can also talk about the Bible verses which your child heard during the meeting: "I will sing praise to you, Almighty God." Psalm 9:2 (GNB); "He made us, and we belong to him." Psalm 100:3 (GNB); "[Jesus said,] 'I love you.'" John 15:9 (GNB).

My Family

Say: "Elizabeth and Zechariah took Baby John to church. They wanted John to grow up to love God. They knew God had a special plan for John." Provide water-based markers or crayons. Guide the preschoolers to complete the picture of Baby John going to the temple for the first time. They may choose to draw any number of things, like a dirt road, houses, the sun, and trees and other plants around Elizabeth and Zechariah.

Roller Prints

PROVIDE

various types of hair rollers (hot rollers, plastic rollers, sponge rollers, etc.), light-colored construction paper, a shallow container of tempera paint, painting smocks, wet paper towels

WHAT TO DO

Put a smock on each child. Allow the preschoolers to have fun making prints on construction paper with mommy's hair rollers. Tell them to press the hair roller in the paint and then on their paper.

Puzzle Frames

PROVIDE

4 craft sticks for each preschooler, 4½-inch cardboard square for each preschooler, fast-drying glue, one box of mini puzzle pieces (purchased from a discount store and boxed in 100- to 250-piece puzzles)

WHAT TO DO

Guide the preschoolers to glue their craft sticks onto their cardboard squares, leaving 2 sides "open" (see illustration). Allow them to decorate their frames however they wish by gluing the puzzle pieces on the craft sticks. Tell them they can put a picture of their family in their frames.

PROVIDE

coffee filters, medicine droppers, 2–3 different colors of food coloring, water, 2–3 small plastic bowls

WHAT TO DO

Put water and a few drops of food coloring in the bowls (one color per bowl). Place bowls and medicine droppers in the middle of the table. Explain to preschoolers that they must drop colored water only on their coffee filters. Guide them to flatten their filters and then drop colored water on the filters. Tell them to watch the colors run into other colors. Ask them if they know what the filters are for and if anyone in their families makes coffee. Talk about how their families take care of them.

Coffee Filters Drip

Parents

Your child may have participated in any one of these activities. You can extend your child's learning by participating in these activities and talking about these Bible verses: "Children, obey your parents." Colossians 3:20 (NIV); "I give thanks to God." 2 Timothy 1:3 (GNB); "Respect your father and your mother." Exodus 20:12 (GNB).

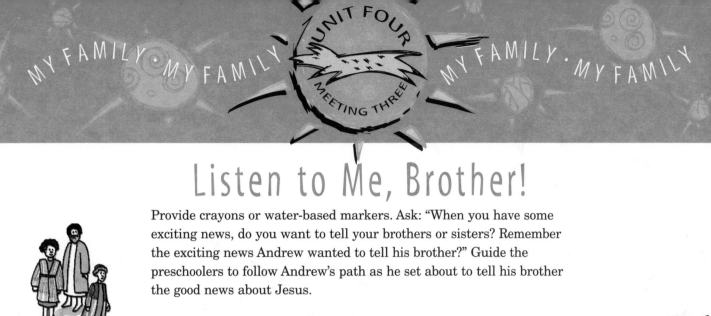

Listen to Me, Brother!

Provide crayons or water-based markers. Ask: "When you have some exciting news, do you want to tell your brothers or sisters? Remember the exciting news Andrew wanted to tell his brother?" Guide the preschoolers to follow Andrew's path as he set about to tell his brother the good news about Jesus.

47

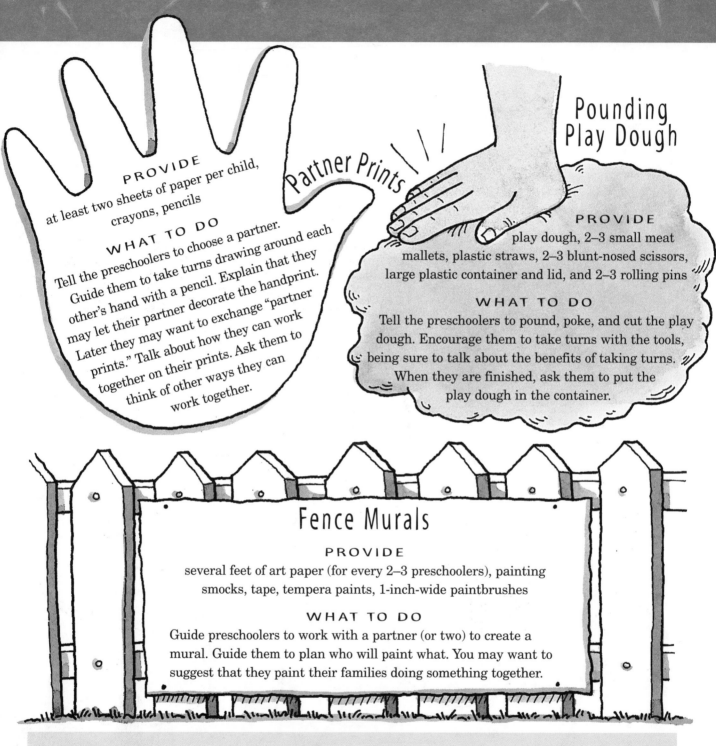

Partner Prints

PROVIDE
at least two sheets of paper per child, crayons, pencils

WHAT TO DO
Tell the preschoolers to choose a partner. Guide them to take turns drawing around each other's hand with a pencil. Explain that they may let their partner decorate the handprint. Later they may want to exchange "partner prints." Talk about how they can work together on their prints. Ask them to think of other ways they can work together.

Pounding Play Dough

PROVIDE
play dough, 2–3 small meat mallets, plastic straws, 2–3 blunt-nosed scissors, large plastic container and lid, and 2–3 rolling pins

WHAT TO DO
Tell the preschoolers to pound, poke, and cut the play dough. Encourage them to take turns with the tools, being sure to talk about the benefits of taking turns. When they are finished, ask them to put the play dough in the container.

Fence Murals

PROVIDE
several feet of art paper (for every 2–3 preschoolers), painting smocks, tape, tempera paints, 1-inch-wide paintbrushes

WHAT TO DO
Guide preschoolers to work with a partner (or two) to create a mural. Guide them to plan who will paint what. You may want to suggest that they paint their families doing something together.

Parents!

Your preschooler may have participated in any one of these activities. You can extend your child's learning by doing these activities at home and by talking about these Bible verses:
"Let us love one another." 1 John 4:7 (NIV); "I give thanks to God." 2 Timothy 1:3 (GNB);
"Respect your father and your mother." Exodus 20:12 (GNB).

What Do Grandparents Do?

Provide crayons or water-based markers. Talk to preschoolers about their grandparents. Guide each child to draw him- or herself between the grandparents. Then direct them to look at the different pictures below and draw lines to the activities they do with their grandparents. *(They may want to draw other activities on another sheet of paper.)*

49

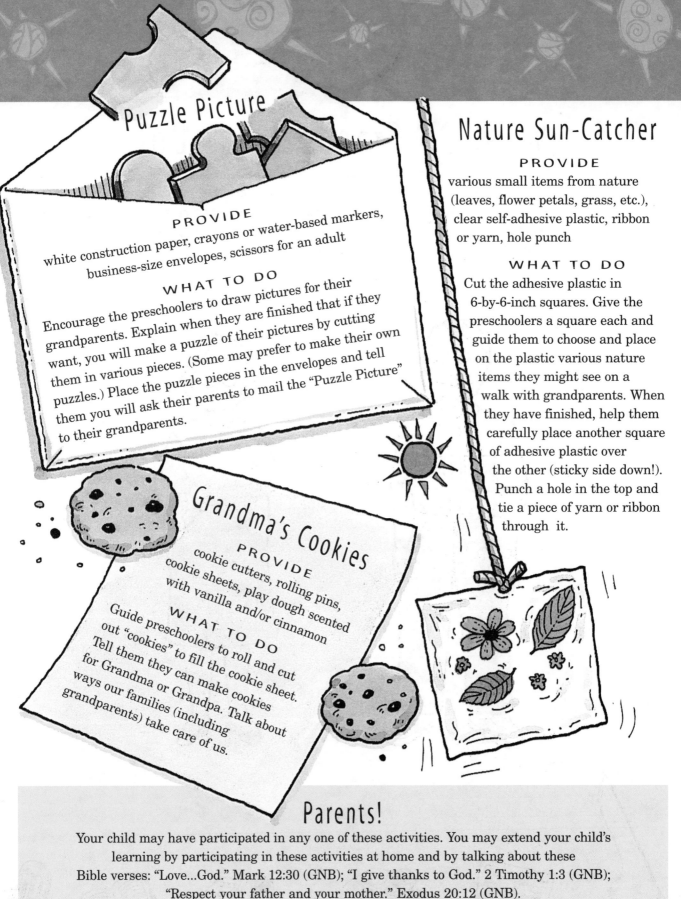

Puzzle Picture

PROVIDE

white construction paper, crayons or water-based markers, business-size envelopes, scissors for an adult

WHAT TO DO

Encourage the preschoolers to draw pictures for their grandparents. Explain when they are finished that if they want, you will make a puzzle of their pictures by cutting them in various pieces. (Some may prefer to make their own puzzles.) Place the puzzle pieces in the envelopes and tell them you will ask their parents to mail the "Puzzle Picture" to their grandparents.

Nature Sun-Catcher

PROVIDE

various small items from nature (leaves, flower petals, grass, etc.), clear self-adhesive plastic, ribbon or yarn, hole punch

WHAT TO DO

Cut the adhesive plastic in 6-by-6-inch squares. Give the preschoolers a square each and guide them to choose and place on the plastic various nature items they might see on a walk with grandparents. When they have finished, help them carefully place another square of adhesive plastic over the other (sticky side down!). Punch a hole in the top and tie a piece of yarn or ribbon through it.

Grandma's Cookies

PROVIDE

cookie cutters, rolling pins, cookie sheets, play dough scented with vanilla and/or cinnamon

WHAT TO DO

Guide preschoolers to roll and cut out "cookies" to fill the cookie sheet. Tell them they can make cookies for Grandma or Grandpa. Talk about ways our families (including grandparents) take care of us.

Parents!

Your child may have participated in any one of these activities. You may extend your child's learning by participating in these activities at home and by talking about these Bible verses: "Love...God." Mark 12:30 (GNB); "I give thanks to God." 2 Timothy 1:3 (GNB); "Respect your father and your mother." Exodus 20:12 (GNB).

Finding My Friends

Provide water-based markers or crayons and paper. Guide the boys and girls to complete the three mazes using a different color for each friend. After they complete the mazes, ask them to name some friends they like to visit (or would like to visit). If they want, write a friend's name below each child on the right side of the paper (or help them write the names if they are able). Encourage the preschoolers to draw things on another piece of paper they like to do with each of their friends or places they like to go with these friends.

57

Flower Friends

PROVIDE
paper plates, crayons or water-based markers, construction paper (half sheets, 5 per child), scissors, gel glue/craft sticks or stapler

WHAT TO DO
Each child should draw her face on the center of the paper plate. Guide preschoolers to cut out 5 flower petals from half sheets of construction paper. (They can just trim off the corners.) On each flower petal they can draw one of the following: 1) what makes them happy, 2) what makes them sad, 3) what makes them angry, 4) what makes them scared, 5) times when they have fun. After they have drawn their pictures, guide them to attach the petals around the rim of the paper plate to make their flowers. Talk about what friends can do for one another in each of these situations.

Friends in the Wind

PROVIDE
construction paper, tape, water-based markers or crayons, yarn, paper ribbon streamers, scissors, stapler

WHAT TO DO
Say: "Wind socks are used to tell us which way the wind is blowing, but they can also be used to identify where things are. We are going to make a wind sock to let our friends know where they can find us." Guide preschoolers to draw pictures of their friends or things they like to do with their friends on the construction paper. Roll the construction paper into a cylinder and tape it. Staple a 12-inch length of yarn to the wind sock at one end. At the other end staple multicolored streamers cut in approximately 2-foot lengths. Talk about places they can hang their wind sock at home.

Friendship Phone

PROVIDE
2 small drinking cups per child (plastic cups are more durable), string, nail, 1-inch pieces of drinking straws, stickers and/or colored tape

WHAT TO DO
Guide preschoolers to decorate their cups with pieces of colored tape and/or various stickers. Turn the cup upside down and allow the child to punch a hole in the bottom of the cup with a nail. Give each child a piece of string (approximately 4 feet long) and guide her to insert it through the hole, pulling it through to the inside of the cup. You probably will need to help the child tie that end of the string around a piece of drinking straw. After following the same procedure for both cups, the phone is complete. Allow the preschoolers to practice talking to each other. While you work on this project, talk about appropriate phone manners to use with friends.

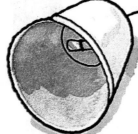

Parents!
Your child has participated in some of these activities during this meeting. You can extend your child's learning by working with him or her on these activities at home. You can also talk about the Bible verses which your child heard during the meeting: "Give thanks to the Lord, because he is good." Psalm 107:1 (GNB); "Friends always show their love." Proverbs 17:17 (GNB); "Jesus said, 'You are my friends.'" John 15:14 (GNB).

Who's Alike?

Provide pencils and water-based markers or crayons. Guide the boys
and girls to circle the child in each group that has a different shirt
from the others. After they have marked them all, direct the boys and
girls to draw a line connecting the two children with matching shirts.
Expand the preschoolers' vocabulary by using phrases like *same,
not the same, alike, different,* and *match, do not match.*

59

New Clothes

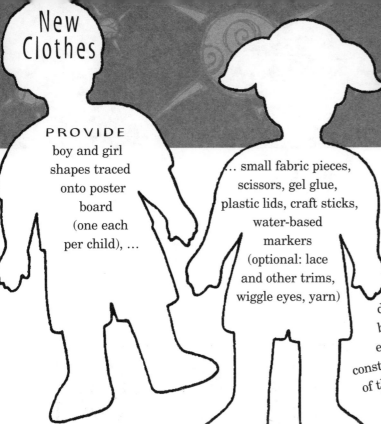

PROVIDE
boy and girl shapes traced onto poster board (one each per child), … small fabric pieces, scissors, gel glue, plastic lids, craft sticks, water-based markers (optional: lace and other trims, wiggle eyes, yarn)

WHAT TO DO

Before the meeting enlarge the boy and girl shapes from this page and trace them onto poster board. Before they begin, preschoolers will need to decide if they are going to dress the boy and girl alike or different. Guide them to glue pieces of fabric on the shapes in a collage form to create their clothing. (Put a little glue on a plastic lid and allow preschoolers to dip into it with the craft sticks.) Some preschoolers may want to add lace and trims. After they are finished gluing, they can add facial features with the markers. If you choose, they can add wiggle eyes and yarn hair. Another option would be to cut out around the shapes, trimming off excess fabric edges to create stand-up figures.

A Friends Stack-Up

PROVIDE
pre-cut white construction paper circles (1½ inches in diameter, 3 per child), water-based markers or crayons, empty toilet tissue tubes, construction paper (cut the width of the tubes), gel glue, craft sticks

WHAT TO DO

Ask the boys and girls to think of 3 of their friends. They are to draw the faces of their friends on the 3 circles, 1 face per circle. On a piece of construction paper, guide them to draw something different they like to do with each of those friends. When they are finished they can glue the construction paper strip around the tube. They can glue the 3 faces on the tube, covering the edges of the paper, stacked from bottom to top. Their "friends stack-up" can help remind them at home to pray for their friends.

Rock Friends

PROVIDE
a number of small rocks and pebbles, pieces of cardboard, gel glue, tempera paint, brushes, hair dryer

WHAT TO DO

Explain to the preschoolers that they are going to create some new friends; no two friends will be just alike, because no two rocks are just alike. Allow the boys and girls to choose their own rocks. They will need 2 for feet, 1 for a body, 1 for a head, and 2 for arms. They can paint them before or after they glue the pieces together to make their "friend." Gluing the "feet" rocks to the cardboard will help to give stability. The hair dryer can be used to help dry the paint and/or glue as necessary. If time permits, they may choose to make more than one "new friend."

Parents!

Your child has participated in some of these activities during this meeting. You can extend your child's learning by working with him or her on these activities at home. You can also talk about the Bible verses which your child heard during the meeting: "Love one another." John 15:17 (GNB); "Friends always show their love." Proverbs 17:17 (GNB); "Jesus said, 'You are my friends.'" John 15:14 (GNB).

Who Is Taking Turns?

Provide blunt-nosed scissors, glue, and water-based markers or crayons. Guide the boys and girls to decorate the happy/sad faces and cut them apart from the side of the page. Guide them to study the pictures and understand what is represented in each set of pictures. Let them glue a happy face on the picture that shows preschoolers taking turns and a sad face where preschoolers are not taking turns.

61

Take Turns Mask

PROVIDE

paper plates, blunt-nosed scissors, water-based markers, construction paper pieces, gel glue, craft sticks/plastic lid

WHAT TO DO

Before you begin explain to the boys and girls how the activity will proceed. Each child will take a paper plate and begin making a mask. The coach will tell everyone to add one feature at a time to the mask. After each feature is added, they will pass the plates around the circle to the left. The coach will say something else to add, and everyone will add that item to his or her neighbor's mask. Then everyone will trade again, and so on. The mask will continue around the circle until it comes back to the original owner. Depending upon the number of children in your group (no more than 5–6), give the following commands: add eyes, mouth, nose, ears, hair, and so forth. Preschoolers can draw or cut the facial features out of construction paper and glue them on.

Friendship Tree

PROVIDE

a small twig for each child, miscellaneous plastic containers, clay, construction paper (cut into fourths), water-based markers, hole punch, paper clips or tape

WHAT TO DO

Allow each child to select a twig and container. Instruct the preschoolers to put a ball of clay in the bottom of the container and to stand the twig in it. Ask them to think of their favorite toy. They are to draw a picture of it on five different pieces of paper (or whatever number of preschoolers there are in the group). Let the preschoolers take turns punching holes at the top of their pictures. Explain how they can take a paper clip and bend it to make a hook. (If there are three's in your group, use tape instead.) They can then take turns hanging one of their favorite toys on each of their friends' trees. Talk about the importance of sharing what you have with your friends.

Gadget Painting

PROVIDE

as many gadgets (potato masher, thread spool, adding machine tape spool, fork, berry basket, etc.) as preschoolers in your group; large construction paper; tempera paint (one color per gadget); pie pan and paper towel (for each color of paint)

WHAT TO DO

Place a paper towel in the bottom of the pie pan. Put a little of the paint on the towel, creating a "stamp pad" for them to press their gadgets on. Give each child a piece of paper and one gadget and paint. Tell the preschoolers that you will say "Trade" in a couple of minutes and they will all switch gadgets. Each child will get a turn with every gadget. Discuss how nice it is for everyone to have a turn.

Parents!

Your child has participated in some of these activities during this meeting. You can extend your child's learning by working with him or her on these activities at home. You can also talk about the Bible verses which your child heard during the meeting: "Be kind and tender-hearted to one another." Ephesians 4:32 (GNB); "Friends always show their love." Proverbs 17:17 (GNB); "Jesus said, 'You are my friends.'" John 15:14 (GNB).

They Helped and I Can Help

Provide pencils, water-based markers or crayons, and paper. Guide the boys and girls to identify the activity represented in each picture. Ask them questions to help them determine if that picture is something from the Bible story or if it could happen today. They can draw a circle around the pictures about the Bible story and a box around the modern-day pictures. When they are finished, encourage them to draw pictures of other ways we can help people today.

63

First Aid Helpers

PROVIDE

12-by-24-inch drawing paper, water-based markers or crayons, blunt-nosed scissors, self-adhesive bandages

WHAT TO DO

Ask, "What did the kind man do for the man who was hurt?" Direct the preschoolers to trace one of their hands and one foot on their paper. Guide them to cut out their hands and feet and to write their names on them. Give each child the same number of bandages as there are children in the group. Tell them to attach a bandage to each of their friends' pictures, either on the hand or foot. Review the Bible story as you complete the activity. Discuss what they can do to help sick or hurt people they know.

Fold-Over Picture

PROVIDE

construction paper, blunt-nosed scissors, water-based markers or crayons

WHAT TO DO

Before the meeting print the verse "Friends always show their love." (Proverbs 17:17) on a piece of construction paper for each child in the group. Fold over the top right corner of the construction paper toward the left edge of the paper to form a triangle. Trim off the remaining portion at the bottom (the bottom 3 inches). This will create square pieces of paper for each child. When the preschoolers gather for this activity, tell them to open the paper out flat and fold the top left corner down to the bottom right. (You may need to fold your own to show them what you mean.) After opening the paper out flat again, they will see an *X* formed by the folds. Show them how to fold all points of the paper to the center, creasing the sides well. Guide them to draw, underneath the flaps, a picture of how they can help a friend. They can decorate the outside of the flaps, also. Some older preschoolers can copy the verse you printed earlier on the outside of one of the flaps. Younger preschoolers may want to trace the letters after you print the verse on the picture for them. Encourage them to show their pictures to a friend. Talk about what the verse means.

Rubber Band Printing

PROVIDE

12-by-24-inch construction paper, juice cans or soup cans (one per child), rubber bands, tempera paint, pie pan and paper towel (one for each child), painting smocks

WHAT TO DO

Before you begin fold the paper towel into the bottom of the pie pan and add a small of amount of tempera on the towel to create a "stamp pad." Explain that the boys and girls can help each other make their pictures. Each child can hold his can while his neighbor places several rubber bands around it. After they have arranged their bands, guide them to roll the can in the paint and then roll it on their paper. They may choose to trade cans and try different colors of paint as they observe the various patterns of the bands. Talk about why it is good to work together.

Parents!

Your child has participated in some of these activities during this meeting. You can extend your child's learning by working with him or her on these activities at home. You can also talk about the Bible verses which your child heard during the meeting: "God loves the one who gives gladly." 2 Corinthians 9:7 (GNB); "Friends always show their love." Proverbs 17:17 (GNB); "Jesus said, 'You are my friends.'" John 15:14 (GNB).

The Five Friends

Provide pencils and water-based markers or crayons. Guide the boys and girls to recall the story and to put the pictures in order by drawing a line from the first one to the next one, and so on. After completing the sequencing activity, they may choose to draw additional background items for each scene represented.

65

Thumb Friends

PROVIDE

construction paper, water-based markers or crayons, stamp pad, hand lotion, moist towelettes

WHAT TO DO

Guide preschoolers to draw a simple "Bible times" house (basically a brown rectangle with a door) on a piece of construction paper. Give each child a drop of hand lotion to rub into her thumb (this will help to clean the ink off afterwards). Guide each child to press her thumb on the ink pad and make her thumbprint at the bottom of the page or inside the house she drew. (Tell her to use the alcohol-based towelette to clean her thumb between prints.) Encourage her to add facial features with the markers. Then ask everyone to pass their papers to the left. They should then put their thumbprints on their neighbor's paper and add their own personal features. Continue this process until every child has added a thumbprint person to all of the pictures. Boys and girls may wish to add other details to the house with the crayons.

Buddy Painting

PROVIDE

12-by-24-inch drawing paper, water-color paint sets, brushes and small containers of water

WHAT TO DO

Help each child pair up with a "buddy." Explain that they will work together on two pictures, one for each child. They can both paint on the first piece of paper, working together to create a picture. Then give them a second piece of paper to create a picture for the other member of the team. Talk about the various aspects of being a friend: friends help, work together, take turns, share, and so forth.

Friendly Fence Weaving

PROVIDE

a chain link fence,
weavable items (about 2 or 3 feet long)
like crepe paper streamers,
fabric strips, rope, ribbon, yarn

WHAT TO DO

Before the meeting find an accessible and safe area of fencing. Tell preschoolers that there are times when it is important to cooperate with other people. (You will probably need to talk about the word *cooperate*.) Tell them it can also be more fun to cooperate with our friends to get a job done. Guide them to work together to weave the section of the fence you have chosen with the materials you have provided. Encourage preschoolers to think of ways they can work with a partner or several other children to create a beautiful piece of art on the fence.

Parents!

Your child has participated in some of these activities during this meeting. You can extend your child's learning by working with him or her on these activities at home. You can also talk about the Bible verses which your child heard during the meeting: "Jesus healed many people." Luke 7:21 (GNB); "Friends always show their love." Proverbs 17:17 (GNB); "Jesus said, 'You are my friends.'" John 15:14 (GNB).

66

Hidden Pictures

Provide crayons or water-based markers. Help preschoolers identify the pictures at the bottom of the sheet. Talk about the Bible story picture. Tell preschoolers the same pictures at the bottom of the sheet are hidden in the big picture. Guide them to find each picture and draw a circle around it.

67

Sponge Paint Stars

PROVIDE
sponges cut in the shape of stars, yellow or white tempera, pie pans, black paper, painting smocks

WHAT TO DO
Mix tempera paint and pour into pie pans. Preschoolers can dip the star-shaped sponges into the paint and press them on their paper. Talk about the nighttime sky and the stars that shone the night Jesus was born. Include the verse "Jesus was born in the town of Bethlehem" (Matthew 2:1) in your conversation.

Jesus and a Manger

PROVIDE
craft sticks (4 per child), poster board, straw or hay, glue, round-head clothespins or small wooden ice cream spoons, water-based markers, white cloth, yarn, clear tape

WHAT TO DO
Cut poster board and cloth into 4-by-4-inch squares. Place art materials on a table. Guide each child to do as much of the activity as he can for himself. Show preschoolers how to glue two sticks together to form an X. Each child will need to glue 2 sets of sticks together. Lay the sticks aside to dry. To make the baby, wrap a small piece of cloth around the clothespin and secure with a piece of yarn. Preschoolers may want to draw a face on the round part of the clothespin. Tell them to fold the poster board squares in half to form a V to make the manger bed. Position the bed between the sticks and tape them together. Put a small amount of straw in the bed and place the baby in the manger. Recall the Bible story with preschoolers as they work.

A Baby Jesus Book

PROVIDE
Muslin, water-based markers, index cards, pinking shears, needle and thread

WHAT TO DO
Cut muslin with pinking shears into 8½-by-11-inch pieces. On index cards print words such as *Mary, Joseph, Baby Jesus, manger, cow, donkey,* and *stars.* Talk about today's Bible story with the preschoolers. Read the word cards to them. Tell preschoolers they are going to make a book about Baby Jesus' birth to give to a younger preschool department. Ask preschoolers to choose a word and draw a picture about that word on a piece of muslin. When each picture is complete, print the word from the card at the bottom. Help preschoolers decide on the order of the pages. Someone may want to make a cover. Stitch the pages together. Deliver the book to a younger preschool department.

Parents!
Your child may have participated in any one of these activities during this meeting. You can extend your child's learning by working with him or her on these activities. You can also talk about the Bible verses which your child heard during the meeting: "Jesus was born in the town of Bethlehem." Matthew 2:1 (GNB); "Jesus said, 'Let the children come to me.'" Matthew 19:14 (GNB); "Jesus...went around doing good." Acts 10:38. (NIV).

Where Is Boy Jesus?

Provide crayons for this activity. Ask each child to place her crayon on the star at the bottom of the path. Begin telling the Bible story at the point where Mary and Joseph discover Jesus is missing. Preschoolers can follow the path with their crayons. Tell the rest of the story, guiding preschoolers to follow the path back to the temple in Jerusalem and then back down the path toward home. Some preschoolers may want to help you tell the story. Emphasize the importance of going to church to learn about God.

69

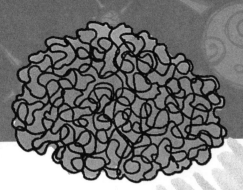

Scouring Pad Painting

PROVIDE
scouring pads, several colors of tempera, manila paper, painting smocks, pie pans

WHAT TO DO
Mix paint and pour in pie pans. Place several scouring pads in each container of paint. Preschoolers can experiment with different ways to move the scouring pad over their paper to make designs. Talk about how they are using their minds to think about different ways to paint and different colors to choose.

Shapes and Sizes

PROVIDE
different colors of construction paper, glue, manila paper, crayons

WHAT TO DO
For threes, cut circles in 3 different sizes from colored construction paper. For older preschoolers, cut different shapes such as circles, squares, rectangles, and triangles. As threes glue circle shapes talk about the different sizes and colors. Older preschoolers can glue shapes in order of size or sort them in various categories. While working, talk about how they are using their minds to think about how to sort the shapes.

Yarn Pictures

PROVIDE
black yarn, crayons or water-based markers, paper, glue in small bottles

WHAT TO DO
Invite preschoolers to draw on their paper with the glue (they can draw whatever they wish). Guide them to place yarn over the glue and when it is dry, to decorate inside the outline. Talk about the fact that Jesus grew and they are growing and can do many things.

Paper Chain

PROVIDE
Various colored strips of paper, glue

WHAT TO DO
Cut paper into 1-inch-wide strips. Show preschoolers how to make a circle from the paper strip, glue it, then loop another one to it to make [chai]n. Guide them to make the chain as long as they [wish. Tal]k about how people grow at different [ ]out how not everyone the

Parents!

Your child may have participated in any one of these activities during this meeting. You can extend your child's learning by working with him or her on these activities. You can also talk about the Bible verses which your child heard during the meeting: "Jesus grew." Luke 2:52 (GNB); "Jesus said, 'Let the children come to me.'" Matthew 19:14 (GNB); "Jesus...went around doing good." Acts 10:38 (NIV).

How Can I Help?

Provide crayons or water-based markers for this activity. Help preschoolers identify and draw a line to the item each person needs. Talk about what these people may and may not be able to do. Decide ways to help the different individuals. Ask preschoolers to match the pictures of the people to what they use to go from one place to another.

71

Scripture Door Hanger

PROVIDE

Poster board, water-based markers, glitter (optional), glue

WHAT TO DO

Before the meeting cut a 9-by-4-inch rectangle for each child from the poster board. Cut a 2½-inch circle about half an inch from the top of each rectangle. Print "*Jesus healed many people.*" (*Luke 7:21*) close to the bottom of the door hanger. Encourage preschoolers to decorate their door hangers. Suggest to the preschoolers that they can give their hangers to a friend who may be sick.

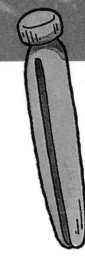

Clothespin Bible People

PROVIDE

Round-head clothespins, water-based markers, fabric scraps, yarn, chenille craft stems

WHAT TO DO

Cut fabric scraps into small squares. Talk about the Bible story for this meeting. Suggest to preschoolers that they make a Bible person they heard about in the story. Demonstrate how to wrap the craft stems around the clothespins to make arms. The fabric can be wrapped around and tied to make clothes. Allow preschoolers to be creative with the materials.

Get Well Cards

PROVIDE

white paper, crayons, water-based markers, construction paper, glue, paper cupcake holders

WHAT TO DO

Preschoolers can use the materials to design "Get Well" or "Thinking of You" cards. Encourage them to think of a message they would like to say. Offer to print the message on the card. Suggest they give the card to a friend.

Parents!

Your child may have participated in any one of these activities during this meeting. You can extend your child's learning by working with him or her on these activities. You can also talk about the Bible verses which your child heard during the meeting:

"Jesus healed many people." Luke 7:21 (GNB);
"Jesus said, 'Let the children come to me.'" Matthew 19:14 (GNB);
"Jesus...went around doing good." Acts 10:38 (NIV).

The Bible Is a Special Book

Provide colored pencils. Show preschoolers your Bible. Talk about why it is special to you. Ask preschoolers to tell you some of their favorite Bible stories (you may need to prompt their memories). Talk about ways to care for our Bibles. Assist preschoolers as needed in following the dots and dashes to complete the picture.

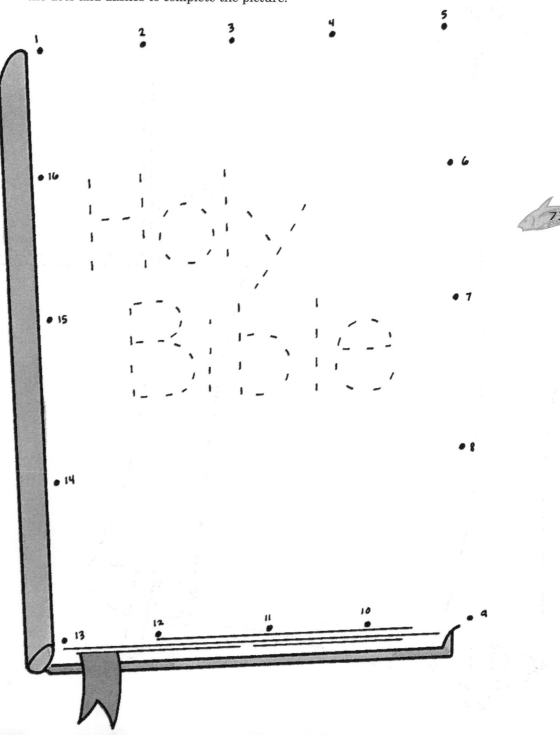

73

Magnet Painting

PROVIDE

magnet strips, paper plates, tempera paint (several colors), paper clips

WHAT TO DO

Mix several colors of tempera paint to a fairly thin consistency. Cut the magnet strips into 2-inch pieces. Spoon or pour paint onto the center of her plate. Place a paper clip in the paint. Tell the child to hold the plate with one hand and the magnet with the other. Place the magnet under the plate close to the paper clip. As the child moves the magnet, the paper clip should move, causing the paint to mix over the plate. Point out the beautiful color(s) on the child's plate. Tell her God made all the beautiful colors and that we learn more about what God made at church.

Stained Glass Windows

PROVIDE

waxed paper, construction paper, glue

WHAT TO DO

Cut a window-shaped frame from black construction paper. Tear or cut several different colors of construction paper into 1-inch pieces. Cut waxed paper the size of the window frame. Provide 2 sheets of waxed paper for each child. Tell preschoolers to choose different colors of paper to glue onto 1 sheet of the waxed paper. Cover the finished piece of waxed paper with the second sheet and glue around the edges. Glue the black frame around the waxed paper to make a stained glass window. Talk about where they might see stained glass windows (at church). Talk about what they learn at church and that Jesus learned at church and He taught others at church.

Bible Scroll

PROVIDE

unsharpened pencils or craft sticks, white paper, tape, yarn, colored pencils

WHAT TO DO

Cut paper into strips a half inch shorter than the pencils or craft sticks. Recall the Bible stories told about Jesus the past few meetings. Encourage preschoolers to pick a favorite story and draw a picture of that story. Offer to print or let the child print the Bible verse that goes with that story. Tape the paper strip to the pencils or craft sticks. Show the preschoolers how to roll the paper to form a scroll. Tie the scroll with a piece of yarn.

Parents!

Your child may have participated in any one of these activities during this meeting. You can extend your child's learning by working with him or her on these activities. You can also talk about the Bible verses which your child heard during the meeting: "Jesus...read the Scriptures." Luke 4:16 (GNB); "Jesus said, 'Let the children come to me.'" Matthew 19:14 (GNB); "Jesus...went around doing good." Acts 10:38 (NIV).

Thank You, God

Provide crayons or water-based markers for this activity. Preschoolers can learn to say thank-you prayers for those things they experience in God's world. They can be thankful for things God has given to them and their families. Talk about the pictures, explaining that something is missing in each picture. At the bottom are the missing pictures. Guide preschoolers to draw a line from the picture to the place that it will fit best. Thank God for each of these things.

75

Thank You, God Circle Book

PROVIDE

white construction paper, crayons or water-based markers, hole punch, metal ring or yarn

WHAT TO DO

Cut five 4-inch circles for each child. Print *Thank You, God* on the first circle of each set. Talk about things for which we can be thankful. Give each child a set of circles. Suggest that he draw pictures of things for which he would like to thank God. Label the pictures for the preschoolers unless they are able to write for themselves. Assist preschoolers in punching holes in their circles and attaching them with a metal ring or yarn.

Nature Collage

PROVIDE

rocks, shells, nuts, leaves, acorns, flowers, glue, tape, heavy paper or cardboard

WHAT TO DO

Arrange the nature items on the table (or take a nature walk and collect items). Allow preschoolers to glue the items on the heavy paper or cardboard. While they work with the materials, talk about the beautiful world God has made.

Mural of God's World

PROVIDE

large sheet of art paper, water colors, brushes

WHAT TO DO

Print the words *God's Beautiful World* at the top of the paper. Talk with preschoolers about the beautiful world God has made for us to enjoy. Suggest to preschoolers they paint a picture of something in God's world. Talk about the grass, flowers, trees, mountains, sun, and sky. Help them plan where these might go on the paper.

Parents!

Your child may have participated in any one of these activities during this meeting. You can extend your child's learning by working with him or her on these activities. You can also talk about the Bible verses which your child heard during the meeting: "Jesus...prayed." Luke 5:16 (NIV); "Jesus said, 'Let the children come to me.'" Matthew 19:14 (GNB); "Jesus...went around doing good." Acts 10:38 (NIV).

Matching Pictures

Provide crayons for this activity. Help preschoolers recall
the Bible story. Look at each row together. Help them decide which
pictures match and draw a circle around the matching pictures.

77

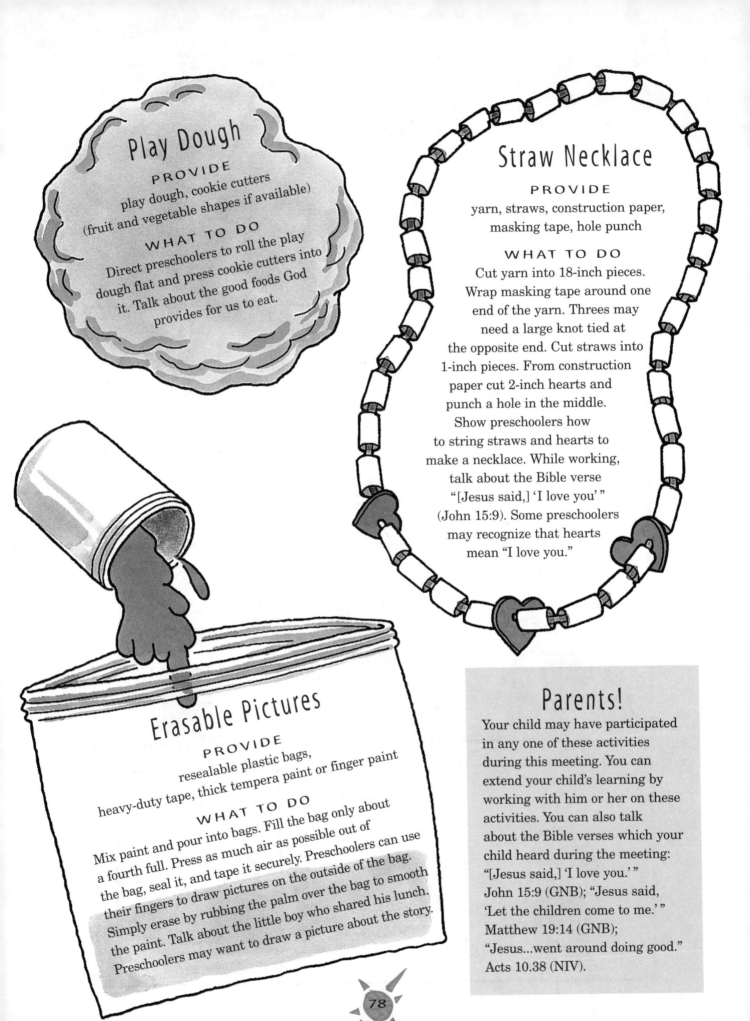

Play Dough

PROVIDE
play dough, cookie cutters (fruit and vegetable shapes if available)

WHAT TO DO
Direct preschoolers to roll the play dough flat and press cookie cutters into it. Talk about the good foods God provides for us to eat.

Straw Necklace

PROVIDE
yarn, straws, construction paper, masking tape, hole punch

WHAT TO DO
Cut yarn into 18-inch pieces. Wrap masking tape around one end of the yarn. Threes may need a large knot tied at the opposite end. Cut straws into 1-inch pieces. From construction paper cut 2-inch hearts and punch a hole in the middle. Show preschoolers how to string straws and hearts to make a necklace. While working, talk about the Bible verse "[Jesus said,] 'I love you'" (John 15:9). Some preschoolers may recognize that hearts mean "I love you."

Erasable Pictures

PROVIDE
resealable plastic bags, heavy-duty tape, thick tempera paint or finger paint

WHAT TO DO
Mix paint and pour into bags. Fill the bag only about a fourth full. Press as much air as possible out of the bag, seal it, and tape it securely. Preschoolers can use their fingers to draw pictures on the outside of the bag. Simply erase by rubbing the palm over the bag to smooth the paint. Talk about the little boy who shared his lunch. Preschoolers may want to draw a picture about the story.

Parents!
Your child may have participated in any one of these activities during this meeting. You can extend your child's learning by working with him or her on these activities. You can also talk about the Bible verses which your child heard during the meeting: "[Jesus said,] 'I love you.'" John 15:9 (GNB); "Jesus said, 'Let the children come to me.'" Matthew 19:14 (GNB); "Jesus...went around doing good." Acts 10.38 (NIV).